To Jan and the Utzon family,

Thank you for your support and endorsement.
We are so pleased to present this book as a
homage to your father and his wonderful work
with the Sydney Opera House.

– C.V. and N.J.

First published 2022

EK Books
an imprint of Exisle Publishing Pty Ltd
PO Box 864, Chatswood, NSW 2057, Australia
226 High Street, Dunedin, 9016, New Zealand
www.ekbooks.org

A CiP record for this book is available from the National Library
of Australia.

ISBN 978-1-922539-14-4

Designed by Mark Thacker
Typeset in Minya Nouvelle 18 on 25pt
Printed in China

This book uses paper sourced under ISO 14001 guidelines from
well-managed forests and other controlled sources.

10 9 8 7 6 5 4 3 2 1

Jørn's Magnificent Imagination

'The architect's gift to society is to bring joy to the people from the surroundings they create.'
— Jørn Utzon

Coral Vass

Nicky Johnston

Jørn loved ideas.

He collected ideas everywhere he went.

Jørn collected ideas
from swans by the lake,

flowers in the meadow,
and seashells on the shore.

Jørn even collected ideas from his orange peels at breakfast.

Jørn loved crafting towers from cardboard boxes,

and bridges from folded paper.

He made forts from sticks and string,

and built cubbyhouses from sheets and blankets.

He even made sailboats from his orange peels at breakfast.

Some said, 'It's odd!'

Some said, 'It's different!'

His teachers didn't
know what to say.

But his parents said,
'It's magnificent!'

As Jørn grew bigger, so did his ideas.

He had ideas about floating buildings and upside-down palaces.

He had ideas for dangling temples and climbing courtyards.

Jørn even had ideas
about overhanging houses
from his orange peels
at breakfast.

Then one day,
Jørn had a new idea.
A magnificent idea.

He set to work.
He studied maps from
across the world.

He examined charts and
diagrams. He researched
ports and harbours.

He drew ...

and he drew ...

and he drew until Jørn
came up with a design.

A grand design.

A *magnificent* design.

Jørn decided to enter his design in a competition.

Not everyone liked his design.

But the judges said, 'It's magnificent!'

'It's genius!'

And Jørn won.

Soon everyone in the world would see Jørn's magnificent design.

At first, people
didn't like it.

Some said, 'It's silly!'

Some said, 'It's ugly!'

Some said, 'It can never be built!'

Others didn't know
what to say.

But the architects said ...

'It's magnificent!
'It's a masterpiece!'

Before long, the workers began building.

Some said, 'It is too hard to build!'

Some said, 'It will take a very long time to build.'

Others even said, 'It will take a lot of money to build.'

But finally, over many days ...
months ... and years, Jørn's design
started to look ... magnificent!

It had shapes like shells and bells,
curves like sails and snails,
and even arches that looked like
orange peels from breakfast.

It was the most peculiar thing
anyone had ever seen.

Word quickly spread over land,
across the seas,
and around the world.

After a while, people forgot they
had ever not-liked Jørn's design.

Some said, 'It looks
like a shell.'

Some said, 'It looks
like a flower.'

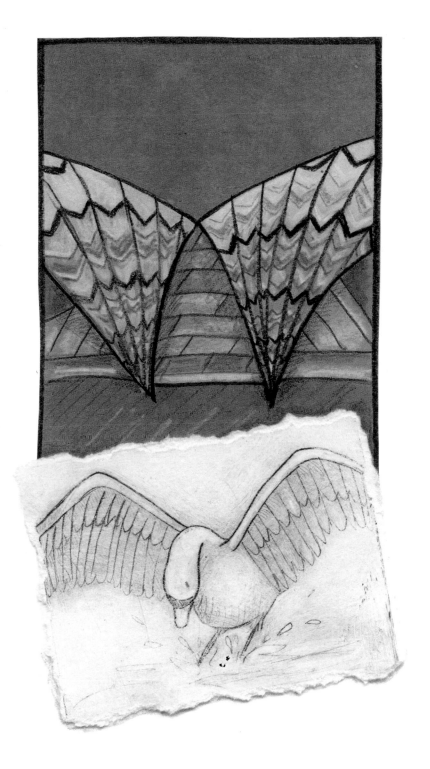

Some even said, 'It looks like a swan'.

Others didn't know what it looked like.

1918
(9 April)
Jørn Utzon is born in Copenhagen, Denmark.

1937
Jørn attends the Royal Danish Academy of Fine Arts.

1942
Jørn graduates as a qualified architect.

1942-46
Jørn works in different drawing offices.

1947-49
Jørn Utzon is inspired as he travels through Europe, Morocco, the United States and Mexico.

1950
Jørn establishes his own practice in Copenhagen.

1952
Jørn builds an open-plan house for himself in Hellebæk, the first of its kind in Denmark.

1957
(January 29)
Jørn Utzon is announced the winner of an international competition to design the Sydney Opera House in Australia.

1957
(July)
The NSW Parliament votes in favour of building Jørn's design.

1959
(2 March)
Construction of the Sydney Opera House begins.

1965
Under a new government, Jørn Utzon's designs, schedules and cost estimates are questioned.